A GIFT FOR:

★ ★ ★ ★ ★ ★ ★ ★ ★ ★ ★ ★ ★ ★ ★

FROM:

★ ★ ★ ★ ★ ★ ★ ★ ★ ★ ★ ★ ★ ★ ★

Design by Mark Voss Design

All images used under license from Shutterstock.com.

ISBN: 978-1-63059-914-0
BOK2280

Made in China
MAY16

TRIVIA AMERICANA

THE ULTIMATE COLLECTION OF MORE THAN 1000 FUN AND FASCINATING TRIVIA QUESTIONS ABOUT THE UNITED STATES

Kennebunkport, Maine

CATEGORIES

★ ★ ★ ★ ★ ★ ★ ★ ★ ★ ★ ★

American History & Geography
Games
Sports
Famous People
Food & Restaurants
Music
State by State

★ ★ ★ ★ ★ ★ ★ ★ ★ ★ ★

AMERICAN HISTORY & GEOGRAPHY

★ ★ ★ ★ ★ ★ ★ ★ ★ ★ ★

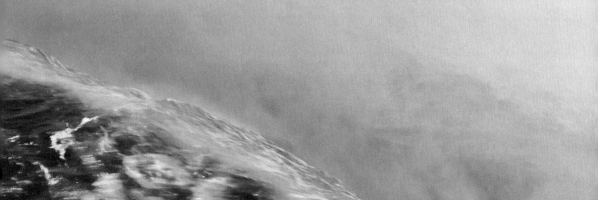

FORGING A NATION

★ ★

In what year was Plymouth settled by the Pilgrims?

In what year was Jamestown established as the first permanent English colony in the New World?

Who wrote the pamphlet "Common Sense" in 1776, arguing that the American colonies needed independence from England?

In what state did the Battles of Saratoga take place in 1777?

After hearing about the American victory in Saratoga, which country joined the Revolutionary War on the patriots' side?

What original colony is NOT bordered by the Atlantic Ocean?

Five men drafted the Declaration of Independence: John Adams, Roger Sherman, Benjamin Franklin, Robert Livingston, and Thomas Jefferson. Which of these men was the sole representative from the South?

In what city was the Declaration of Independence printed?

Who was the first to sign the Declaration of Independence?

Who was the primary author of the Declaration of Independence?

What country invaded Washington, D.C., in 1814?

Who led the Continental Army troops across the Delaware River into New Jersey in 1776?

In what city was the Constitution of the United States written?

When the Constitution was first written, what were its supporters called?

Answers: Philadelphia, John Hancock—because he was president of Congress, Thomas Jefferson, England, George Washington, Philadelphia, Federalists

Where was the Declaration of Independence stored
for safekeeping during World War II?

Who was the principal author of the
Constitution of the United States?

John Adams and Thomas Jefferson died
on the same date in 1826. What day?

What man is known for riding through the night,
announcing the British army's advance toward
Lexington and Concord?

Who was the first man to be killed in the Boston
Massacre and, therefore, in the Revolutionary War?

Who is known for creating the first American flag
for General George Washington?

During the Revolutionary War, Emily Geiger kept a secret military message from the British. When she was captured, how did she destroy the message?

Whose face is on the $100 bill?

What military figure from the Revolutionary War has a name that has become synonymous with betrayal?

Which state's leaders refused to participate in the convention to write the Constitution of the United States?

What are the first ten amendments of the Constitution of the United States known as?

Who served as the first vice president and second president of the United States?

PRESIDENTS

Who is the only president to be elected
unanimously by the electoral college—twice?

What is the minimum age to be elected
president of the United States?

How many presidents were awarded the
Nobel Peace Prize?

On what holiday did Eleanor marry
Franklin D. Roosevelt in 1905?

Following the assassination of John F. Kennedy,
who became our 36th president?

Which president starred in 53 films before being
elected governor of California?

"Tippecanoe and Tyler Too" refers to which
presidential and vice presidential running mates?
a) William Howard Taft and James S. Sherman
b) Bill Clinton and Al Gore
c) Woodrow Wilson and Thomas R. Marshall
d) William Henry Harrison and John Tyler

Who was the 2nd U.S. president?
a) Benjamin Franklin
b) Thomas Jefferson
c) John Adams
d) John Quincy Adams

Which of the following presidents did NOT
receive a college degree?
a) Harry S. Truman
b) George W. Bush
c) James Monroe
d) Theodore Roosevelt

Which President did NOT serve in the Civil War?
a) William McKinley
b) Ulysses S. Grant
c) Abraham Lincoln
d) Rutherford B. Hayes

Which U.S. President got stuck in the
White House bathtub?

Answers: C, A – one of eleven presidents total, C – he was a captain in the Black Hawk War of 1832, William Howard Taft.

What state holds the first primary in the quadrennial U.S. presidential election cycle?

Who is the only person who served as a U.S. president and then a Supreme Court justice?

Who was the smallest U.S. president, never weighing more than 100 pounds?

Who was the first president to hold a televised press conference?

Who served the shortest presidency?

Who was the first president to shake hands with guests?

★ ★ ★ ★ ★ ★ ★ ★ ★ ★ ★ ★ ★ ★ ★ ★ ★ ★ ★ ★

FUN FACT

Millions of gallons of water rocket over
Niagara Falls every minute,
about 750,000 gallons each second!

★ ★ ★ ★ ★ ★ ★ ★ ★ ★ ★ ★ ★ ★ ★ ★ ★ ★ ★ ★

GEOGRAPHY & GEOLOGY

Where is Old Faithful?
a) Nebraska
b) North Dakota
c) Washington
d) Wyoming

How long did it take for plants to start growing again after the eruption of Mount St. Helens?
a) Days
b) Weeks
c) Months
d) Years

What does the letter in an iceberg's name refer to?
a) Its weight
b) Its height
c) Its depth
d) Its place of origin

About how long is the U.S.
continental coastline?

a) 100,000 miles

b) 200,000 miles

c) 250,000 miles

d) 350,000 miles

Which of the following states doesn't have the
Mississippi River running through it?

a) Mississippi

b) Missouri

c) Indiana

d) Maryland

The SS *Edmund Fitzgerald* sank in
Lake Superior in what year?

a) 1945

b) 1955

c) 1965

d) 1975

The Great Salt Lake covers
how many square miles?

a) 170

b) 1,700

c) 17,000

d) 170,000

Is the Atlantic Ocean growing or shrinking?

In what state is Siesta Beach, considered by some to be the best beach in the U.S.?

In what state are Wildwood, North Wildwood, and Wildwood Crest beaches?

In what state is Kauapea Beach?

In what state is Ocracoke Island Beach?

In what state is Wildcat Beach?

In what state is Poipu Beach?

In what state is Sanibel Island?

In what state is South Padre Island?

In what state is Catalina Island?

In what New England state is Old Orchard Beach?

In what Pacific state is Cannon Beach?

In what state is Malibu Beach?

In what state is Galveston Beach?

In what state is Panama City Beach?

In what state is Cape Hatteras?

Oval Beach is located in what Midwest state?

In what state is the source of the Mississippi?

Which is closer to the source of the Mississippi: Genoa, Wisconsin, or Hannibal, Missouri?

The Savanna-Sabula Bridge connects Savanna, Illinois to the island of Sabula, which is part of what state?

America's oldest state park is at what water feature?

What New York State river is named after an English explorer?

What river forms a border between Virginia and Maryland?

How many of the five largest lakes in the world are Great Lakes?

Toledo, Ohio, is on what Great Lake?

Traverse City, Michigan, is on what Great Lake?

Thunder Bay, Ontario, is on what Great Lake?

Duluth, Minnesota, is on what Great Lake?

Rochester, New York, is on what Great Lake?

Green Bay, Wisconsin, is on what Great Lake?

Which of the Great Lakes is at a lower elevation than the others?

The Straits of Mackinac connect which two Great Lakes?

The St. Marys River connects which two Great Lakes?

Georgian Bay is part of what Great Lake?

Which Great Lake is entirely within the United States?

The names of which two Great Lakes come from French words?

NATURAL DISASTERS

In what state did the strongest U.S. earthquake occur?
a) California
b) New Mexico
c) Hawaii
d) Alaska

What American city was burned to the ground in 1871 in a fire allegedly started by a cow?
a) Atlanta
b) Chicago
c) Cincinnati
d) San Francisco

What hurricane devastated New Orleans in 2005?
a) Hugo
b) Katrina
c) Rita
d) Wilma

What hurricane struck New Jersey in 2011,
the first to hit that state in more than a century?
a) Andrew
b) Ike
c) Irene
d) Wilma

Which caused more deaths, the Great Chicago Fire
or Wisconsin's Peshtigo Fire (which happened on
the same day)?

Which has more people killed by fires each year,
Russia or the United States?

Which has more people killed by fires each year,
Finland or the United States?

What was the first volunteer fire company,
founded by Ben Franklin, called?
a) Union Fire Company
b) First Union Company
c) First Anti-Fire Brigade of the United States
d) The U.S. Fire and Emergency Company

In 1941, the Terminal Hotel burned in what city?
a) Charlotte
b) Cleveland
c) Atlanta
d) Baltimore

What city had the first full-time paid
fire department in the U.S.?
a) Philadelphia
b) Boston
c) Washington, D.C.
d) Cincinnati

AMERICAN HISTORY & GEOGRAPHY
LIGHTNING ROUND

True or false: Six months after the American colonies declared independence from England, they elected George Washington as the first president of the United States.

True or false: George Washington used a thermometer and a weather vane to gauge the weather and made note of the measurements in his diary.

True or false: George Washington served ice cream to guests.

True or false: Harry S. Truman's middle name was Shippe.

True or false: As first written, the Constitution counted enslaved persons as three-fifths of a free person.

True or false: The Mississippi River was once the border between the Spanish Empire and the British Empire.

True or false: There's a 37-mile-long magma chamber under New York City.

True or false: There are places on the Mississippi River that are more than 180 feet deep.

True or false: More than half of Idaho is covered in trees.

True or false: New Smyrna Beach is right next to Old Smyrna Beach.

True or false: The name Mississippi comes from a Greek word.

True or false: The Pontchartrain Causeway is the longest bridge over water in America.

True or false: Amerigo Vespucci was the first European to reach the Mississippi River.

True or false: Water skiing was invented on the Mississippi River.

True or false: The Hoover Dam is the only dam on the Colorado River.

True or false: The Great Salt Lake is about 75 miles long.

True or false: The Great Salt Lake in Utah is over 200 feet deep in places.

True or false: There are no islands on the Great Salt Lake.

True or false: Few fish live in the Great Salt Lake.

True or false: It is estimated that over 100 billion brine flies make their home at the Great Salt Lake.

True or false: The combined Great Lakes are larger than New York and New Jersey combined.

True or false: The highest peak in the Adirondacks is Mount Milly.

True or false: The Appalachians stretch
from Quebec to Alabama.

True or false: In 2003, a hailstone was found
that had a circumference over 18 inches.

True or false: In 1947, the temperature in the
Yukon Territory reached -81°F.

★ ★ ★ ★ ★ ★ ★ ★ ★ ★ ★ ★ ★ ★

GAMES

★ ★ ★ ★ ★ ★ ★ ★ ★ ★ ★ ★ ★

BOARD & CARD GAMES

Robert Angel invented Pictionary
while living in what state?

What does the orange "A" square on a Pictionary game
board require you to draw if you land there?

The game Battleship was first released by Milton
Bradley in what year?
a) 1911
b) 1932
c) 1945
d) 1967

What is the name of the Queen (later changed to a Princess) in Candy Land?

In Othello, who makes the first move, light or dark?

How many pawns does each player get in a game of Sorry!?

How many points do you need to score in the upper section of Yahtzee in order to get a bonus?

How many pairs of pants are in a game of Ants in the Pants?

How many monkeys do you need to hook together to win a game of Barrel of Monkeys?

How many pieces are there in a total Cootie?

How many buckets in a game of Hi Ho! Cherry-O?

What is the highest hand in poker
(with no wild cards)?

What beats paper in Rock Paper Scissors?

Is the game Landslide about presidential politics
or natural disasters?

How many white checkers start out a game
of Backgammon in red's home board?

Are the players in Apples to Apples dealt
green apple cards or red apple cards?

How much time does it take a Pictionary
timer to run out?

What color Cranium spaces let players choose a category?

How many points do you get in Balderdash if you guess the correct definition?

Where is the corporate headquarters of beloved game company Hasbro?

What do you have to do in order to play a shorter game of Scene It?

How many continents are on the Risk board?

What does the name of the popular game Pente mean in Greek?
a) Pants
b) Five
c) Shape
d) People

Which is not the color of an Uno card?
a) Red
b) Orange
c) Green
d) Blue

Which of the following games is NOT played
by Bill and Ted against Death in *Bill & Ted's
Bogus Journey*?
a) Twister
b) Battleship
c) Candy Land
d) Electronic football

Which of the following games is NOT currently
produced by American toy and game company
Hasbro?
a) Trivial Pursuit
b) Slamwich
c) Jenga
d) Cranium
f) Clue

FUN FACT

In 2011, a game of Dodge Ball
at the University of California, Irvine,
included more than 4,400 players.

DUNGEONS & DRAGONS

In Dungeons & Dragons, what is an NPC?

In Dungeons & Dragons, what is a D20?

Who leads a game of Dungeons & Dragons?
a) The oldest player
b) The Dungeon Master
c) The Cerberus
d) The Leading Troll

What Oscar winner starred in the movie
Dungeons & Dragons?
a) Daniel Day-Lewis
b) Anthony Hopkins
c) Jeremy Irons
d) Ben Kingsley

In what Rona Jaffe novel does a troubled
college student become dangerously obsessed
with a Dungeons & Dragons-like game?
a) *Lizards and Labyrinths*
b) *Mazes and Monsters*
c) *Treasures and Trolls*
d) *Witches and Warriors*

What famous American action movie star
is a professed Dungeons & Dragons fan?

Created by American game designers Gary
Gygax and Dave Arneson, the game was first
published in what year?

THE GAME OF LIFE

What are the two choices you have when
starting The Game of Life?
A) "Get Married" or "Stay Single"
B) "Buy a Car" or "Rent a Car"
C) "Start a Career" or "Start College"
D) "Buy, Buy, Buy!" or "Sell, Sell, Sell!"

Which of the following houses can
you NOT buy?
A) Seaside Abode
B) Tudor
C) Log Cabin
D) Country Cottage

How many numbers on The
Game of Life spinner?

What is the largest denomination of cash
in The Game of Life?

What was added in the 1990s?

a) The option of staying single

b) Life Tiles, which rewarded good behavior

c) Gambling in retirement

d) The option to travel backward

In the early editions of The Game of Life,
Art Linkletter appeared on its cover.
Who was Art Linkletter?

a) A baseball player

b) A former governor

c) A New York real estate mogul

d) A TV game-show host

Which of the following was NOT featured
in a special edition of The Game of Life?

a) *Monsters, Inc.*

b) *Indiana Jones*

c) *The Wizard of Oz*

d) *The Chronicles of Narnia*

CROSSWORD PUZZLES

In a crossword puzzle, which clues are usually listed first, the across clues or the down clues?

Which tends to have more letter squares in a same-size puzzle, an American-style crossword grid or a British-style crossword grid?

When did *The New York Times* begin
publishing crossword puzzles?
a) 1942
b) 1955
c) 1960
d) 1964

What puzzle popularizer founded the American
Crossword Puzzle Tournament?
a) Will Geer
b) Will Pants
c) Will Shortz
d) Will Shertz

Simon & Schuster published the first book
of crossword puzzles in 1924 with what
attached to it?

What do you call a person who loves
crossword puzzles?

MONOPOLY

Name the four Monopoly railroads.

Which of the following was NOT once
a Monopoly piece:
a) Lantern
b) Purse
c) Sled
d) Rocking horse

In what movie do characters play Monopoly
with real money?
a) *Night of the Living Dead*
b) *Zombieland*
c) *Shaun of the Dead*
d) *Return of the Living Dead*

Do you know Monopoly's official subtitle?

How much money is in a
Monopoly game box?
a) $10,540
b) $14,500
c) $20,580
d) $26,665

Which space on the board is landed on the
most?
a) Go
b) Jail
c) Illinois Avenue
d) Boardwalk

What American game company was first to
mass-market Monopoly?
a) Hasbro
b) Ideal
c) Milton Bradley
d) Parker Brothers

PLAYGROUND & BACKYARD GAMES

How much corn (in pounds) should fill the bags used in the popular American lawn game "cornhole"?

How many points do you get in cornhole for landing a bag in the hole?

How many holes in a standard wiffle ball?

What happens in dodgeball if you catch a ball thrown at you?

The Four Square World Championship is held in...
a) Maine
b) Minnesota
c) Maryland
d) Mississippi

How large is the official Four Square
league ball?
a) 3.5 inches
b) 5.5 inches
c) 8.5 inches
d) 12.5 inches

In the United States, what's another name for
croquet hoops?
a) Archdoors
b) Wickets
c) Tunnels
d) Bats

Wiffle ball was invented in the...
a) 1920s
b) 1930s
c) 1950s
d) 1970s

What is the color of a typical wiffle ball bat?
a) Yellow
b) White
c) Orange
d) Red

FUN FACT

A 1982 song called "Pac-Man Fever"
became a top-10 record.

What's another name for a close shoe
in horseshoes?

a) A neary

b) An incher

c) A shoe in count

d) An almost

In cornhole, what is a "Carlton"?

a) When a bag hits the ground then rolls
   or bounces onto the board.

b) When a bag knocks an opponent's bag
   into the hole

c) When all four bags land in a hole in
   an inning

d) When a team scores no points in an inning

In ladder toss (also known as ladder golf
or hillbilly golf), what are the strung-together
balls called?

a) Boleros

b) Bojos

c) Bolas

d) Bohos

ELECTRONIC GAMES

What gaming system was the Halo video game released for?

In Call of Duty: Modern Warfare 3, what country invades the United States?

Where do the Sims live?

Which came first: Xbox One or Xbox 360?

Zynga has developed all of the following games except:
a) The Sims
b) Zynga Poker
c) FarmVille
d) Words with Friends

Which of the following artists does NOT have
a hit song of his or hers featured on the first
Rock Band?
a) Red Hot Chili Peppers
b) Kiss
c) Madonna
d) The Police

What year was strategy video game
Age of Empires released?
a) 1999
b) 1997
c) 1996
d) 1998

What 1981 video game was about getting
a frog to cross the road?

What classic board game was
Words with Friends based off of?

LIGHTNING ROUND

True or false: Many 1,000-piece jigsaw puzzles actually have more than 1,000 pieces.

True or false: All 1,000-piece jigsaw puzzles have the same pattern of pieces, only with different illustrations.

True or false: Early jigsaw puzzles were actually cut by a fret saw, not a jigsaw.

Answers: True, False, True

True or false: During the Great Depression, there were companies that issued weekly jigsaw puzzles.

True or false: Boggle was created by the same person who created Scrabble.

True or false: Sales of Twister took off after it was played on "The Tonight Show."

True or false: Canasta is played with 152 cards.

True or false: Domino spots are sometimes called Peps.

True or false: Eucre is played with 32 cards.

True or false: Zynga, the company that created FarmVille, is headquartered in San Francisco, California.

True or false: **Scrabble tiles are made from the wood from elm trees.**

True or false: **A losing player at the World Scrabble Championship once accused his opponent of pocketing a G and demanded that officials strip-search him.**

True or false: **The Game of Life was originally titled The Checkered Game of Life.**

True or false: **Escape maps were hidden in Monopoly sets that were sent to American prisoners of war during World War II.**

True or false: **The prize at the Monopoly World Championships is the real dollar equivalent of the amount of fake money in a Monopoly game box.**

True or false: **In the movie *The Sting*, Robert Redford switches a gangster's stash of cash with a sack of Monopoly money.**

True or false: **Aggie, Mica, and Cat's Eye are all types of marbles.**

True or false: **Horseshoe stakes should be positioned straight up.**

True or false: **In early kickball, there was a pitcher.**

True or false: **The Atari was the first home video game system.**

True or false: **In Civilization IV, Abraham Lincoln was one of the original world leaders.**

True or false: **According to the official rules of Monopoly, if all the houses or hotels in the box have been purchased, you can use pennies for houses and nickels for hotels.**

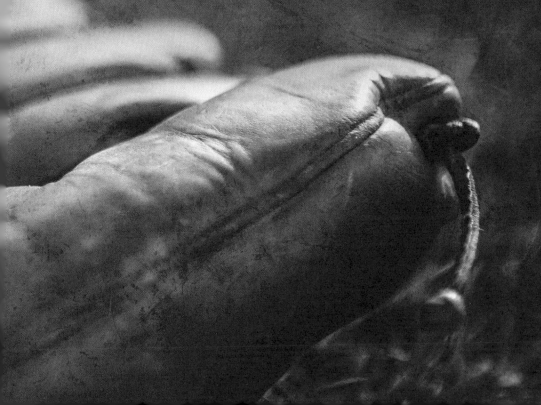

BASEBALL

Who dismissed Giants manager Mel Ott with the phrase, "Nice guys finish last," before replacing him as manager?

Where did the Washington Nationals play before moving to Washington?

Who was the first African-American manager
to win the World Series?

What pitching feat has been achieved by, among
others, Charlie Robertson, Len Barker, Dallas
Braden, and David Wells?

Who was the first Rookie of the Year?

Who won the first Cy Young Award?

Where did the Los Angeles Dodgers play
before moving to Los Angeles?

What three brothers played the outfield together
for three innings in 1963?
a) Felipe, Matty, and Jesus Alou
b) Ken, Clete, and Cloyd Boyer
c) Joe, Dom, and Vince DiMaggio
d) Ed, Jim, and Tom Delahanty

Match the nickname to the player:

1) The Count   a) Roger Bresnahan
2) The Duke of Flatbush   b) John Montefusco
3) The Duke of Tralee   c) Babe Ruth
4) The Red Baron   d) Duke Snider
5) The Sultan of Swat   e) Rick Sutcliffe

Match the player to his uniform number.

1) Mickey Mantle   a) 3
2) Willie Mays   b) 7
3) Pete Rose   c) 14
4) Babe Ruth   d) 24

Where did the Oakland A's play immediately before moving to Oakland?

The New York Yankees have won more World Series than any other team. What team ranks second?

a) Cardinals
b) Dodgers
c) Giants
d) Red Sox

What Hall of Famer was nicknamed
"The Splendid Splinter"?
a) Joe DiMaggio
b) Sandy Koufax
c) Mickey Mantle
d) Ted Williams

What team was the first to win the World Series
after finishing last the previous season?
a) 1914 Braves
b) 1969 Mets
c) 1991 Twins
d) 1997 Marlins

The leftfield wall in what ballpark is known
as "The Green Monster"?
a) Coors Field
b) Dodger Stadium
c) Fenway Park
d) Yankee Stadium

★ ★

FUN FACT

George Francis "Doc" Medich got a head start
on his medical career while still a Major League
player with the Texas Rangers (1972-1982).
The ball player/medical student went out into the stands
to help a fan having a heart attack—on two occasions!

★ ★

Who is the only player to win the batting
championship in three different decades?
a) George Brett
b) Ty Cobb
c) Tony Gwynn
d) Ted Williams

Who coined the phrase, "It ain't over 'til it's over"?
a) Yogi Berra
b) Dizzy Dean
c) Satchel Paige
d) Casey Stengel

How many no-hitters did Roger Clemens pitch?
a) 0
b) 1
c) 2
d) 3

Who was the first National Leaguer to
hit 50 homers in a season?
a) George Foster
b) Ralph Kiner
c) Willie Mays
d) Hack Wilson

What disability was shared by Browns outfielder
Pete Gray and Angels pitcher Jim Abbott?
a) Blindness
b) Deafness
c) Muteness
d) One arm

What is the record for runs scored in one inning?
a) 5
b) 17
c) 25
d) 35

After his retirement, Jackie Robinson became
an executive for what coffee company?
a) Chock Full o' Nuts
b) Folger's
c) Maxwell House
d) Starbucks

What did Ted Williams do in his final at-bat?
a) Single
b) Double
c) Triple
d) Homer

FOOTBALL

Who are the only brothers to both be drafted with the number one pick?

What Oakland Raiders owner was commissioner of the AFL?

Answers: Peyton and Eli Manning, Al Davis

What quarterback "guaranteed" a Super Bowl
victory for the underdog New York Jets,
and then delivered?

Pro Bowl receiver Art Monk is a second cousin
of what jazz legend?

Who led the NFL in rushing yards every year but
one from 1957 to 1965?

The original Cleveland Browns left Cleveland
and are now what team?

What award is given to the top college football
player in the nation?

USC's Roy Riegels and the Minnesota Vikings'
Jim Marshall are both notorious for committing
what blunder?

Astroturf was originally developed for use in what stadium?

The answer to the previous question wasn't the first field to have it installed though. That was Franklin Field, then home to what team?

Match the team to its stadium.
1) Arrowhead Stadium   a. Kansas City Chiefs
2) Levi's Stadium   b. San Francisco 49ers
3) FedEx Field   c. Tennessee Titans
4) Nissan Stadium   d. Washington Redskins

What team won the first two Super Bowls?
a) Chicago Bears
b) Dallas Cowboys
c) Green Bay Packers
d) Pittsburgh Steelers

What is the only team in the Super Bowl
era to go undefeated?
a) Baltimore Colts
b) Indianapolis Colts
c) Miami Dolphins
d) New England Patriots

What team was the first to go 0-16 in a season?
a) Detroit Lions
b) Indianapolis Colts
c) Kansas City Chiefs
d) Tampa Bay Buccaneers

What was Brett Favre's first NFL team?
a) Atlanta Falcons
b) Green Bay Packers
c) Minnesota Vikings
d) New York Giants

What was William Perry's nickname?
a) The Refrigerator
b) The Toaster
c) The Burner
d) The Microwave

What Chicago Bears great was nicknamed "Sweetness"?
a) Dick Butkus
b) Walter Payton
c) Brian Piccolo
d) Gale Sayers

Who was one of the NFL's first African-American players?
a) Jim Brown
b) Tony Dungy
c) Fritz Pollard
d) Jackie Robinson

Future President Ronald Reagan played what Notre Dame football legend in a movie?

a) Grover Cleveland Alexander

b) George Gipp

c) Paul Hornung

d) Knute Rockne

How long has Pat Patriot been the fictional mascot of the New England Patriots?

a) Since 1950

b) Since 1961

c) Since 1972

d) Since 1990

What is the name of the Pittsburgh Steelers' mascot?

a) Steely McIron

b) Steely McSteel

c) Steely McBeam

d) Steely McStuds

BASKETBALL

Did the American Basketball Association
last more or less than a decade?

What colors were the ABA basketball?

What team did Shaquille O'Neal and Kobe
Bryant play for together?

Who had more NBA field goals in a single season, Kareem Abdul-Jabbar or Wilt Chamberlain?

Who had more NBA field goals in a single season, Michael Jordan or Bob McAdoo?

When were the Harlem Globetrotters founded?
a) 1927
b) 1945
c) 1955
d) 1968

Who had more free throws in a single NBA season, Jerry West or Wilt Chamberlain?

Who had a higher NBA career average of steals per game, Michael Jordan or Allen Iverson?

What school has won the most NCAA championships?

What college team did John Wooden
coach from 1948-1975?
a) NYC
b) UCLA
c) LSU
d) USC

What future U.S. senator led Princeton
to the Final Four?

In what year was the three-point
field goal introduced?
a) 1980
b) 1986
c) 1992
d) 1995

How many schools participated in the first
NCAA tournament?
a) 8
b) 16
c) 32
d) 64

HOCKEY

What country did the U.S. team defeat in 1980
to win the Olympic Gold medal?

What arena is home to the New York Rangers?

Answers: Finland, Madison Square Garden

What hockey team, throughout the 1970s, played
Kate Smith's version of "God Bless America" for
the Broad Street Bullies and their fans?

There was no winner of the 1919 Stanley Cup.
Why not?
a) Flu epidemic
b) Player strike
c) World War I
d) The Cup wasn't created 'til 1920

Which of these hockey leagues never competed
for the Stanley Cup?
a) East Coast Hockey League
b) National Hockey Association
c) Pacific Coast Hockey Association
d) Western Canada Hockey League

What's a nickname for the penalty box
with a religious connotation?

BOXING

Gene Tunney beat Jack Dempsey for the world heavyweight championship in 1926. Who won when they fought again in 1927?

In what round did Joe Louis knock out Max Schmeling in their 1938 bout?

What was Muhammad Ali's former name?

What long-shot underdog shocked the boxing world by knocking out Mike Tyson, ending his run as heavyweight champ?

Which heavyweight champ was the father and namesake of a Pro Bowl linebacker for the Cowboys and 49ers?

Who came first, Sugar Ray Leonard or Sugar Ray Robinson?

The movie made about boxer James J. Braddock was called...
a) *A Cinderella Story*
b) *Cinderella Man*
c) *Punching Cinderella*
d) *Cinderella's Fight*

How long did Mike Tyson's 1995 bout against Peter McNeeley last?
a) Two hours, twelve minutes
b) One hour, twelve minutes
c) Twelve minutes
d) One minute, twenty-nine seconds

Sugar Ray Robinson's success prompted what musician to change his name to avoid confusion, using his middle name professionally?

Who fought title bouts against George Foreman and Larry Holmes and won both?
a) Evander Holyfield
b) Muhammad Ali
c) George Foreman
d) Sugar Ray Leonard

In what state did the 1965 title fight between Muhammad Ali and Sonny Liston take place?
a) Maine
b) Massachusetts
c) South Dakota
d) Wyoming

Which heavyweight champ was the father and namesake of a Pro Bowl linebacker for the Cowboys and 49ers?

GOLF

What month is national golf month?

What golfer has a lemonade/iced tea drink named after him?

The Masters is played in what city?

What color jacket do Masters champions wear?

What is the term for scoring two below par
on a hole?

What is the term for scoring three below par
on a hole?

What is the term for scoring two above par
on a hole?

What is the term for scoring three above par
on a hole?

The climax of the movie *Tin Cup* takes place
at what golf tournament?

Who was the youngest player to make an
LPGA cut, at age 16?

Who won the first Solheim Cup match?

American men's golfers compete with European golfers every other year for what trophy?

What is the equivalent trophy for a similar competition among women's golfers?

The first golf match to be televised happened in…
a) New York
b) Atlanta
c) St. Louis
d) San Francisco

Tiger Woods' real first name is:
a) Earl
b) Eldrick
c) Vincent
d) Tiger

VOLLEYBALL

In what year was beach volleyball added
to the Olympics?
a) 1984
b) 1988
c) 1992
d) 1996

Is volleyball a sport in the Paralympics?

How many players on each side in a
volleyball game?

What was the first country besides the U.S.
to embrace volleyball?
a) France
b) Mexico
c) Canada
d) England

Indoor volleyball was created by William G. Morgan, a YMCA physical education director in what state?

What was the original name of volleyball:
a) Volley Squash
b) Mintonette
c) Net Ball
d) Serve and Set

What pair of women took home the gold medal for the U.S. in beach volleyball at the 2012 summer Olympics held in London?

In what state did beach volleyball originate?

SPORTS LIGHTNING ROUND

BASEBALL

True or false: **The Atlanta Braves were once known as the Eagles.**

True or false: **The Los Angeles Dodgers were once known as the Robins.**

True or false: **If the catcher drops strike three, the batter can run to first unless there are less than two outs and a runner on first.**

True or false: **Babe Ruth's real first name was George.**

True or false: **Hank Aaron and Lou Gehrig have the same first and middle names.**

True or false: **In baseball, no one is credited as the winning or losing pitcher in a forfeited game.**

True or false: **In baseball, statistics from a forfeited game do not count.**

True or false: **Babe Ruth once pitched a no-hitter.**

True or false: **Joe Torre, who reached 14 straight postseasons as a manager, never played a postseason game as a player.**

BOXING

True or false: **In 1988, bare-knuckle boxer John L. Sullivan had a match that lasted 75 rounds.**

True or false: **Sugar Ray Robinson won 69 of his 85 amateur bouts by knockouts.**

True or false: **Rocky Marciano never lost a fight.**

FOOTBALL

True or false: **No Super Bowl has ever gone into overtime.**

True or false: **The Pittsburgh Steelers are the only team to win three straight Super Bowls.**

True or false: **A New York Giants quarterback was a contestant on the reality show *The Bachelor*?**

Answers: True, True, True, False—no team has, True

True or false: **Carl Weathers, who played Apollo Creed in the *Rocky* movies, was once a professional football player.**

BASKETBALL

True or false: **Basketball was invented by the head of the P.E. department at a school in Massachusetts when he was asked to create a game to be played in winter.**

True or false: **In early women's basketball, there were a limited number of dribbles a player could do.**

True or false: **The backboard was added to the game to prevent interference from spectators.**

True or false: **It was against the rules to slam dunk between 1967 and 1976.**

HOCKEY

True or false: **The first hockey puck was square.**

True or false: **An NHL hockey puck is made of vulcanized rubber.**

True or false: **Hockey pucks are frozen before put in play.**

True or false: **There are three officials in an NHL hockey game—two referees and a linesman.**

True or false: **There is a regulation size ice rink in the Hockey Hall of Fame.**

SOCCER

True or false: **The United States played in the first World Cup.**

True or false: **Iran once beat the U.S. in a World Cup match.**

True or false: **The World Cup was held despite World War II.**

True or false: **The first Women's World Cup was held in 2000.**

True or false: **Since 1984, professional soccer players have been allowed to compete in the Olympics.**

★ ★ ★ ★ ★ ★ ★ ★ ★ ★ ★ ★ ★ ★ ★ ★

FAMOUS PEOPLE

★ ★ ★ ★ ★ ★ ★ ★ ★ ★ ★ ★ ★ ★ ★ ★

ALSO KNOWN AS

Stefani Germanotta is better known as whom?

What actress, born Diane Hall, was the mother in the *Father of the Bride* movies?

Frederic Austerlitz Jr. is better known as what famous dancer?

Leslie L. King Jr. is better known as what
former U.S. President?

Allan Stewart Konigsberg is better known
as what writer/actor/director?

John Mellencamp's first four albums were
recorded under what name?

What is singer Fergie's full name?

Samuel Clemens is better known as whom?

Katheryn Hudson is better known as what singer?

Phineas Taylor and James Anthony
were the given names of what
famous pair of businessmen?

Match the presidential pairs
to the correct relationship.
1) The Adamses   a) father and son
2) The Harrisons   b) grandfather and grandson
3) The Johnsons   c) cousins
4) The Roosevelts   d) not related

Who is writer William Sydney Porter
better known as?
a) O. Henry
b) Mark Twain
c) Stephen King
d) R. L. Stein

Norma Jean Baker is better known as whom?

Who changed his name to Chad Ochocinco?

What basketball player changed his name
to Metta World Peace?

WHAT'S MY JOB

John Lasseter: Arizona congressman
or head of Pixar?

David Petraeus: CIA director or
building designer?

Augusta Savage: Sculptor or
ten-year fugitive?

Jackie Ormes: award-winning poet
or cartoonist?

Dave Barry: Humor writer or founder
of Amazon.com?

Christopher Buckley: Magazine editor or
Republican presidential candidate?

Fred Gwynne: football commentator
or actor?

Van Cliburn: Pianist or silent-movie actor?

Chuck Close: Former astronaut or
photo-realist painter?

Jon Corzine: U.S. senator or Olympic bobsledder?

Freeman Dyson: Physicist or
infomercial pitchman?

Ira Glass: Radio broadcaster or juggler?

Seymour Hersh: Investigative reporter
or convicted embezzler?

Daniel Handler: Former New York City mayor
or children's book author?

Arianna Huffington: Website cofounder or
cast member of Desperate Housewives?

Judith Jamison: Choreographer
or fashion designer?

Richard Bachman: Pseudonym for Stephen King
or chairman of Southwest Airlines?

Alice Paul: women's rights activist
or scientist?

Janet Napolitano: U.S. Secretary of Homeland
Security or American folksinger?

Jim Morrison: Rock musician or
Harry Truman's vice president?

FUN FACT

Ill-fated aviation pioneer Amelia Earhart
promoted a line of travel bags called
Modernaire Earhart Luggage.

Richard Rorty: Physician or philosopher?

Richard Allen: Methodist minister
or founder of Harvard?

Joseph Stiglitz: Economist or ecologist?

Ansel Adams: Astronomer or photographer?

Kelly Miller: Beatles manager
or mathematician?

Ty Cobb: MLB outfielder
or inventor of the Cobb Salad?

Gloria Steinem: Engineer
or feminist?

Stephen Ambrose: Historian or jockey?

Lydia Chapin Taft: First woman to fly in space or first woman to vote?

Dian Fossey: Gorilla researcher or fashion designer?

Enrico Fermi: Scientist or chef?

Howard Hughes: Reclusive billionaire or magazine publisher?

Sandra Day O'Connor: Suffragette or Supreme Court justice?

John Updike: Plymouth Rock pilgrim or 20th-century American writer?

Henry Luce: Founder of *Time* magazine
or Las Vegas-based magician?

Charles L. Reason: Mathematician or
notorious embezzler?

Jack Welch: Chairman of GE or
creator of the War of the Worlds hoax?

Marsden Hartley: Artist or
animal rights activist?

Billy Mays: Commercial pitchman
or baseball star?

Charles Addams: Cartoonist or
signer of the Declaration of Independence?

Henry David Thoreau: Political philosopher
or Broadway actor?

Pat Garrett: College basketball coach
or killer of Billy the Kid?

August Wilson: Playwright or
creator of the standardized calendar?

Henry Highland Garnet: Abolitionist or
New York mayor?

Ambrose Burnside: Civil War general
or New England poet?

Philip Glass: Early fashion model
or composer?

Neal Adams: Illustrator or adventurer?

William Rollins: X-ray pioneer
or Soviet prisoner/author?

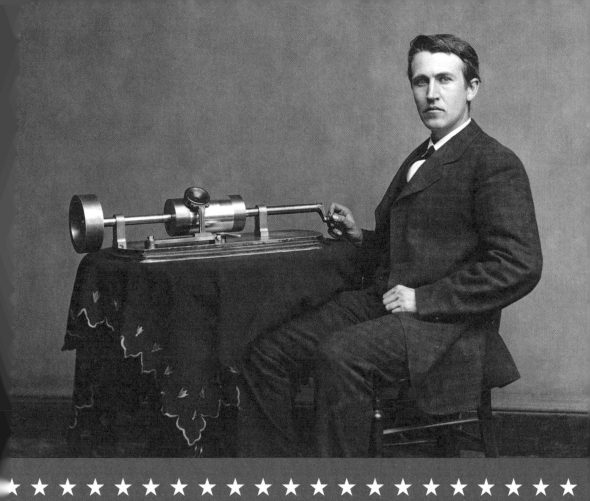

FUN FACT

Thomas Edison's many inventions included
the phonograph, which revolutionized sound
recording even though Edison himself
was hard of hearing.

Margaret Mead: Ethnologist or inventor
of Jell-O?

John Gotti: Mobster or Los Angeles mayor?

Anna Quindlen: Columnist/novelist or
infomercial spokesperson?

Jeff Bezos: Amazon.com founder or
early TV clown?

Bobby Fischer: Kennedy relative
or chess champion?

Brian Wilson: Leader of Irish revolutionary
organization or leader of The Beach Boys?

Biddy Mason: Entrepreneur
or inventor of the nasal strip?

Pierre Omidyar: Political leader
or founder of eBay?

Lon Chaney: Olympic wrestler
or horror-movie star?

Sam Kinison: Comedian or
early motion-picture pioneer?

Louise Fitzhugh: Sports announcer
or best-selling novelist?

Steve Allen: Original host of *The Tonight Show*
or World Series of Poker champion?

Elizabeth Arden: Principal in the movie
Grease or beauty industry pioneer?

Clark Gable: film heartthrob or
founder of Bloomingdales?

Idina Menzel: Singer or congresswoman?

Barbara Billingsley: Creator of the Post-It note
or 50s TV mom?

Ivan Davis: Pianist or Antarctic explorer?

Bonnie Parker: Thief or American model?

Stephen Decatur: War of 1812 naval officer
or founder of Illinois?

Hank Greenberg: Baseball player
or creator of the Snickers Bar?

Gene Krupa: Track and field star or drummer?

Nancy Lopez: Golfer or
New Mexico congresswoman?

Tom Mix: Animal rights activist
or movie cowboy?

James Edward Oglehorpe: Founder of Savannah,
Georgia, or conflicted Wall Street inside trader?

Barry Goldwater: Conservative political icon
or steamboat inventor?

Hal Roach: Movie producer or drug lord?

★ ★

FUN FACT

Civil War hero Ulysses S. Grant so detested the
sight of blood that rare steak nauseated him.

★ ★

Soupy Sales: TV comedian or
Campbell's cofounder?

Don Shula: Legendary acting coach
or football coach?

Madame C.J. Walker: Hair care entrepreneur
or World War II historian?

Douglas Wilder: Virginia governor
or inventor of the microwave?

David Foster Wallace: Novelist
or attempted presidential assassin?

Melvil Dewey: Muppeteer or
developer of library organization system?

Harlan Fiske Stone: Fast-food pioneer
or Supreme Court Chief Justice?

Charles G. Dawes: *Survivor* winner
or U.S. vice president?

Eddie Rickenbacker: Race-car driver
or basketball player?

Johnnie Cochran: Lawyer or
original cast member of *The Electric Company*?

Irv Bauer: Chef or theater critic?

Bob Kane: Batman creator
or fictional newspaper publisher?

Jeb Magruder: Civil War general
or Watergate conspirator?

Claude Shannon: Novelist or mathematician?

Paul Krugman: Actor or economist?

Andrew Wyeth: Artist or signer of
the Declaration of Independence?

Allen Drury: Novelist or TV host?

Pete Sampras: Member of congress
or tennis player?

Vincent Gallo: Actor-director or chemist?

Melvin Belli: Attorney or mobster?

Stephan Pastis: Cartoonist or
Linkedin.com founder?

Craig Newmark: Craigslist founder
or hotel-chain owner?

CELEBRITY NICKNAMES

What baseball player is nicknamed A-Rod?

What baseball player was nicknamed K-Rod?

What NBA player was nicknamed T-Mac?

What musician is nicknamed T-Bone?

What NBA player was nicknamed K-Mart?

St. Louis Cardinals' reliever Marc Rzepczynski is nicknamed after what game?

What baseball player was nicknamed D-Train?

What was William Cody's nickname?

Henry Clay was known as The Great...
a) Henry C
b) Complainer
c) Compromiser
d) Consolidator

Tommy Hearns was known as The...
a) Rat
b) Fox
c) Mouse
d) Beast

Louis Armstrong's nickname was...
a) Satchel
b) Satchmo
c) Salami
d) Scando

What was Stonewall Jackson's real first name?
a) Timothy
b) Truman
c) Thomas
d) Theodore

Baseball great Joe DiMaggio was known
as the _____ Clipper.
a) Clippy
b) Yankee
c) Philly
d) Husky

Joe Namath was nicknamed after what street:
a) Broadway
b) Main Street
c) Broad Street
d) Avenue of the Americas

What was the nickname of jazz great
Charlie Parker?
a) Fly
b) Bird
c) Bee
d) Bug

What American was known as the
father of his country?

What actor and former governor had
the nickname the Governator?

What actor/wrestler is known as the Rock?

What basketball player was
nicknamed Sir Charles?

Who is nicknamed the Hoff?

What band was nicknamed the Most Dangerous Band in the World?

Whose nickname is J.Lo?

What country music great was called the Man in Black?

What is Alfred Matthew Yankovic's nickname?

What silent-movie star was known as the Little Tramp?

Who was known as Honest Abe?

What was Matoaka better known as in American history?

★ ★

FUN FACT

The Susan B. Anthony dollar, a coin honoring
the well-known suffragist, was produced
only from 1979 to 1981 and in 1999.
The vending machine industry wasn't a fan
of a coin too easy to confuse with a quarter.

★ ★

★ ★ ★ ★ ★ ★ ★ ★ ★ ★ ★ ★

FOOD&

RESTAURANTS

★ ★ ★ ★ ★ ★ ★ ★ ★ ★ ★ ★

BREAKFAST

Which was NOT an original flavor of Pop-Tarts?
a) Strawberry
b) Brown sugar cinnamon
c) Apple currant
d) Cherry

What cereal has Tony the Tiger as a mascot?

Pop-Tarts were once advertised with a toaster character named...
a) Marvin
b) Milton
c) Muggsy
d) Manny

What company produces Cheerios?
a) General Mills
b) Kellogg's
c) Kashi
d) None of the above

In what state is Battle Creek, home of Kellogg's?

What is Cap'n Crunch's full name?

Wheaties advertises itself as
"The Breakfast of _____."

Who has been on more different Wheaties boxes:
Tiger Woods or Michael Jordan?

FAST FOOD

Which burger chain had the first deal with Lucasfilm to sell *Star Wars* glasses?

What California-based burger chain, with restaurants in just five states, is famous for a menu limited to the burger, the cheeseburger, and the double-double?

Where is the Taco Bell Arena?
a) Boise, Idaho
b) Cleveland, Ohio
c) Springfield, Illinois
d) West Chester, Pennsylvania

Col. Sanders' first name was...
a) Harry
b) Harrison
c) Henry
d) Harland

True or false: Before he founded Wendy's, Dave Thomas helped create the spinning bucket sign for Kentucky Fried Chicken.

Dave Thomas named Wendy's after his eight-year-old daughter, who was nicknamed Wendy. What was her real name?
a) Betty Lou
b) Melinda Lou
c) Annie Lou
d) Wanda Lou

Hardee's is a sibling of what other restaurant chain?
a) Bob's Big Boy
b) Carl's Jr.
c) Jack in the box
d) Rally's

In what year did Subway begin offering $5 foot-long sandwiches?
a) 1978
b) 1988
c) 1998
d) 2008

The first McDonald's restaurant opened in …
a) 1933
b) 1940
c) 1949
d) 1954

Who is the mayor of McDonaldland?

Match the catchphrase to the fast food chain.
1) Where's the beef?
2) Eat fresh
3) What you crave
4) Home of the Whopper
5) Finger lickin' good
6) Think outside the bun
7) I'm lovin' it.

a) White Castle
b) Kentucky Fried Chicken
c) Burger King
d) Subway
e) Wendy's
f) Taco Bell
g) McDonald's

In what book does the character
Long John Silver appear?

What was Long John Silver's job?

What does Burger King call its coffee?

What presidential candidate swiped the slogan
"Where's the beef?" to attack his main opponent
in the Democratic primaries?
a) Bill Clinton
b) Michael Dukakis
c) Gary Hart
d) Walter Mondale

What chicken restaurant chain is famously
closed on Sundays?
a) Chick-fil-A
b) Church's
c) KFC
d) Popeyes

What Midwestern burger chain
received an unsolicited testimonial from
film critic Roger Ebert in a column,
and posted it, in full, in the drive-thru lane?

Who founded McDonald's?
a) Ray Buktenica
b) Ray Kroc
c) Ray Romano
d) Ray Stevens

The owner of McDonald's also owned what
Major League baseball team?
a) Milwaukee Brewers
b) San Diego Padres
c) San Francisco Giants
d) Texas Rangers

Detroit Red Wings owner Mike Ilitch owns
what pizza chain?
a) Domino's
b) Little Caesars
c) Papa John's
d) Pizza Hut

FUN FACT

In 1926, Frances E. Coffey
made blueprints for the precurser
to the modern-day hot dog cart.

In the song "Jack and Diane," the title characters are "sucking on a chili dog" outside what fast-food restaurant?

On what day do U.S. and Canada 7-Elevens offer free 7.11-ounce Slurpees?

Which of the following has been used in the title of a Hollywood film?
a) KFC
b) White Castle
c) Papa John's
d) Burger King

What building was White Castle restaurants' architecture adapted from?
a) The Empire State Building
b) Westminster Abbey
c) Elsinore
d) Chicago Water Tower

How many White Castle hamburgers
are in a Crave Case?

Whose first store was in Hoboken, New Jersey:
Blimpee or Subway?

What Atlanta-based bowl game
has Chick-fil-A sponsored?

What kind of animal is seen in most
Chick-fil-A advertising?

On what holiday does Nathan's Famous
hold its annual hot dog eating contest?

How much time do contestants in the Nathan's
Famous hot dog eating contest have to eat
as many hot dogs as they can?

Do they have to eat the buns?

CHAIN RESTAURANTS

What does TGI Friday's claim the TGI stands for?

Is Chicken Bryan served at Romano's Macaroni Grill or Carrabba's Italian Grill?

Was Outback Steakhouse founded in the 1970s, 1980s, or 1990s?

Where does the Outback Bowl take place?

How many pegs in the peg game on the tables at Cracker Barrel?

Bubba Gump Shrimp Company was inspired by a reference in what Oscar-winning film?

What is the name of the mascot for Red Robin?

Which came first: Hard Rock Café or
Planet Hollywood?

If you are at a Hoss's Steak and Sea House
are you more likely to be in Pennsylvania
or North Dakota?

Ruby Tuesday was founded by five
students from...
a) Harvard
b) The University of Tennessee
c) UCLA
d) M.I.T.

Which of the following is an offering at
Longhorn Steakhouse?
a) Fred's Filet
b) Frieda's Filet
c) Flo's Filet
d) Fern's Filet

★ ★

FUN FACT

Necessity is the mother of invention.
At the 1904 World's Fair in St. Louis,
an ice cream vendor ran out of paper dishes
but was near a vendor of rolled waffles.

★ ★

Which burger chain was a majority investor
in Chipotle from 1998 to 2006?

a) McDonald's

b) Burger King

c) Wendy's

d) Hardee's

Where is the Hard Rock's museum,
the Vault, located?

a) Orlando

b) London

c) Hollywood

d) New York

Which of the following was not one of the original backers of Planet Hollywood?

a) Sylvester Stallone
b) Clint Eastwood
c) Demi Moore
d) Arnold Schwarzenegger

Which of the following was not an unsuccessful spin-off of Planet Hollywood?

a) Cool Planet
b) Marvel Mania
c) Pizza Planet
d) Official All Star Café

How many flavors of ice cream did Howard Johnson's boast of having during its early days?

a) 12
b) 18
c) 28
d) 36

Which of the following is an iconic International House of Pancakes breakfast entrée?

a) Rough and Tumble Fresh 'N Funny
b) Rooty Tooty Fresh 'N Fruity
c) Really Tasty Fun 'N Fancy
d) Crisp and Crunchy Yum to my Tummy

What is the core food at Famous Dave's?

a) Hamburgers
b) Chicken
c) Tacos
d) Barbecue

IHOP's slogan was "Come hungry, leave _____."

What color, traditionally, are the roofs of Howard Johnson's?

SWEET STUFF

The first Pez dispenser sold in America featured what on top?
a) A Ford automobile
b) A Mickey Mouse head
c) Santa Claus
d) The White House

Which of the following was NOT one of the historical figures who topped Pez dispensers in honor of the Bicentennial?
a) Betsy Ross
b) Paul Revere
c) Ben Franklin
c) Daniel Boone

What yellow-wrapped, chocolate-covered peanut bar was Hershey's second product, after the Hershey bar?

According to Mr. Owl, how many licks does it take to get to the center of a Tootsie Pop?

Before undergoing a name change, what were milk chocolate M&M's called?

What candy was prominently featured in the movie "E.T."?

Bart Simpson has appeared in commercials for what candy bar?

Match the slogan to the breath freshener:
1) Brush your breath   a) Altoids
2) The curiously strong mints   b) Certs
3) The 1½ Calorie Breath Mint   c) Dentyne
4) Two-two-two mints in one   d) Tic Tac

What candy bar is named after a novel by Alexandre Dumas?

Appropriately, what candy company manufactures the Milky Way bar?

What brand of bubble gum comes with a comic strip inside the wrapper?

What is the current name of the candy bar once called the $100,000 Bar?

What chocolate-covered nougat bar was named after a popular dance?

What candy bar features a bee on the wrapper?

The name of what candy bar is short for "twin sticks"?

What chewing gum has frequently advertised itself using twin sisters as spokesmodels?

What do you get if you combine chocolate, marshmallows, and graham crackers?

FUN FACT

Hershey's Kisses were introduced in 1907.
Their name might have been inspired by
the sound of the chocolate being deposited
during manufacturing.

What was introduced at the 1904 World's Fair
in St. Louis?
a) The first ice cream sundae
b) Sprinkles/jimmies
c) Neapolitan ice cream
d) The edible cone

Which of the following does not claim to be the
place where the ice cream sundae was created?
a) Two Rivers, Wisconsin
b) Hoboken, New Jersey
c) Ithaca, New York
d) Evanston, Illinois

The chocolate-covered ice cream bar,
the Eskimo Pie, was launched in 1934 in the
city of Onawa. What state is Onawa in?
a) Ohio
b) Indiana
c) Iowa
d) Idaho

SODA

When did soda vending machines
initially appear?
a) 1900s
b) 1920s
c) 1940s
d) 1960s

Which came first, Coca-Cola Cherry or
Caffeine-Free Coca-Cola?

What is the caramel coloring in Coke?
a) E150d
b) F120s
c) L110m
d) N170r

Did Pepsi Blue last more or less than five years?

Was "It's the Real Thing" a Coke or Pepsi slogan?

Was "You Got the Right One, Baby"
a Coke or Pepsi slogan?

Which came first, Sprite or 7-Up?

Which did David Naughton do first: Star in
a singing Dr. Pepper commercial or star in the
movie *An American Werewolf in London*?

Which of the following was NOT a spokesperson
for Pepsi products?
a) Michael Jackson
b) Ray Charles
c) Britney Spears
d) Paul McCartney

What flavor is Mountain Dew Typhoon?
a) Grape
b) Strawberry-pineapple
c) Apple-grape
d) Watermelon

★ ★

FUN FACT

7-Up was originally
Bib-Label Lithiated
Lemon-Lime Soda.

★ ★

FOOD & RESTAURANTS
LIGHTNING ROUND

True or false: Waldorf Salad was named after Archduke Ferdinand Waldorf.

True or false: If you only have one, it's still Pop-Tarts, not Pop-Tart.

True or false: **The same animator who developed Rocky & Bullwinkle also developed the Cap'n Crunch character.**

True or false: **The W.K. Kellogg Foundation was created in 1906 in an effort to help hospital patients digest food.**

True or false: **The first athlete to be featured on a Wheaties box was Babe Ruth.**

True or false: **There wasn't a football player on the front of a Wheaties box until 1986.**

True or false: **There was a cereal called Bill & Ted's Excellent Cereal.**

True or false: **Millenios were Cheerios that included pieces shaped like 2s.**

True or false: **Corn Pops is different in the U.S. than it is in Canada.**

True or false: **Quaker Oats Company is owned by PepsiCo.**

True or false: **Grape-Nuts contains neither grapes nor nuts.**

True or false: **A song called "Dance the Slurp" was given away at 7-Eleven stores in 1970.**

True or false: **A toy whistle included as a prize in boxes of Cap'n Crunch could be used to make long-distance phone calls for free.**

True or false: **To open the first Pizza Hut restaurant, co-owners Frank and Dan Carney borrowed money from their mother.**

Answers: True, True, True, True, True, True

True or false: **Captain Kangaroo star Bob Keeshan was the first Ronald McDonald.**

True or false: **White Castle was founded in Wichita, Kansas.**

True or false: **Jersey Mike's Subs was originally called Mike's Submarines.**

True or false: **Chick-fil-A claims to have introduced the chicken nugget.**

True or false: **Popeyes began as a restaurant called Chicken on the Run.**

True or false: **The original Applebee's was called T.J. Applebee's Rx for Edibles & Elixirs.**

True or false: **The first Cheesecake Factory was in Beverly Hills, California.**

True or false: **Maggiano's Little Italy restaurants were founded in Chicago.**

True or false: **Romano's Macaroni Grill is headquartered in Trenton, New Jersey.**

True or false: **Johnny Carrabba co-founded Carrabba's Italian Grill.**

True or false: **Red Lobster calls its lower-fat choices LightHouse Selections.**

True or false: **There is a National Mustard Museum.**

True or false: **Joe's Crab Shack was founded in Maryland.**

True or false: **Outback Steakhouse was founded in Texas.**

True or false: **There are over 1,800 calories in an Outback Steakhouse Bloomin' Onion.**

True or false: **The first Longhorn Steakhouse was in Atlanta.**

True or false: **Longhorn Steakhouse serves an appetizer called Texas Tonion.**

True or false: **There are no Howard Johnson's restaurants left west of the Mississippi River.**

True or false: **The Oh Henry! Bar is named for Hank Aaron.**

True or false: **Ketchup can be used to shine gold.**

True or false: **Reggie Jackson once had a candy bar named after him.**

True or false: **Six people died from eating Pop Rocks candy combined with soda.**

True or false: **The formula for Coca-Cola is in a bank vault.**

True or false: **Pepsi was first launched as Brad's Drink.**

True or false: **Dr Pepper is named after its creator, Philo T. Pepper.**

True or false: **Jelly Belly makes Dr. Pepper jelly beans.**

True or false: **7-Up has had the same formula since the 1940s.**

★ ★

FUN FACT

Mountain Dew has been marketed
as "game fuel" because of its
popularity among gamers.

★ ★

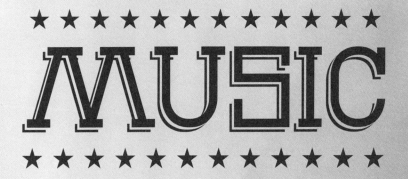

PATRIOTIC SONGS

In "This Land is Your Land," the singer saw the
endless skyway above. What was seen below?

Where are people supposed to face if
"The Star Spangled Banner" is playing
and there is no flag visible?

What is the correct title of the song which begins, "My country, 'tis of thee"?

Who wrote "Stars and Stripes Forever"?

A lot of orchestras play this Tchaikovsky work on the Fourth of July, but it's not inspired by the American Revolution but by a different war. What's the work called?

"The Star Spangled Banner" was written about the attack on Fort McHenry, which overlooks what body of water?
a) Delaware River
b) Chesapeake Bay
c) Atlantic Ocean
d) Gulf of Mexico

When did "The Star Spangled Banner" become the U.S. National anthem?
a) 1922
b) 1931
c) 1940
d) 1954

How high up the Billboard Hot 100 chart
did Whitney Houston's 1983 version of
"The Star Spangled Banner" climb?
a) Number 6
b) Number 12
c) Number 20
d) Number 40

Which comedienne stirred up controversy when
she spit after singing "The Star Spangled Banner"
at a Padres baseball game?
a) Lucille Ball
b) Roseanne Barr
c) Phyllis Diller
d) Sarah Silverman

When did Jimi Hendrix begin
performing his electric guitar version of
"The Star Spangled Banner"?
a) 1964
b) 1966
c) 1969
d) 1970

Who messed up the lyrics to "The Star Spangled
Banner" before Super Bowl XLV?
a) Christina Aguilera
b) Britney Spears
c) Fergie
d) Mama Cass

Daniel Rodriguez' post-9/11 version of
"God Bless America" made it onto the Billboard
Hot 100. What was Rodriguez's regular job?
a) Firefighter
b) Police officer
c) Ambulance driver
d) Construction worker

Who benefits from royalties for the song
"God Bless America"?
a) Girl Scouts and Boy Scouts
b) Keep America Beautiful
c) The American Red Cross
d) The estate of Irving Berlin

FUN FACT

Sales of "You're a Grand Old Flag"
sheet music topped one million copies.

Where was Katharine Lee Bates
a professor when she wrote the lyrics
for "America the Beautiful"?

a) Princeton

b) Harvard

c) Wellesley

d) University of Delaware

Who performed a duet with Ray Charles
of "America the Beautiful" on his Genius
& Friends album?

a) Martina McBride

b) Alicia Keys

c) Amy Winehouse

d) Cobie Caillat

What Broadway show featured the song
"Yankee Doodle Dandy"?

a) Show Boat

b) Oklahoma!

c) 1776

d) Little Johnny Jones

Answers: C—although she was teaching summer classes at Colorado College, B, D

POP & ROCK

Who sang "Respect" (1967)?

Who sang "Hotel California" (1976)?

Who sang "I Want It That Way" (1999)?

Who sang "Where Did Our Love Go" (1964)?

Who sang "Sunday Morning" (2002)?

Who sang "Superstition" (1972)?

Who sang "Everlong" (1997)?

How many Mamas and how many Papas were
there in the Mamas and the Papas?

How many members are there in the Black Keys?

Which of the following is not a Beach Boys song?
a) "Goin' Surfin'"
b) "Surfin' USA"
c) "Surfer Girl"
d) "Surfin' Safari"

Which of the Monkees resisted
any reunion tours?
a) Micky
b) Michael
c) Davy
d) Peter

Which of the following was NOT a song
on the Train album *Train*?
a) "Meet Virginia"
b) "I Am"
c) "Iowa"
d) "Free"

What is the name of Eminem's alter ego?
a) Slappy Sandy
b) Slim Shady
c) Slime Sally
d) Slum Sammy

Which of the following artists did
Kanye West NOT produce for?
a) Alicia Keys
b) Ray Charles
c) Ludacris
d) Janet Jackson

Which of the following did NOT have a song on
the first *Now That's What I Call Music* disc?
a) Hanson
b) Lenny Kravitz
c) Madonna
d) Imajin

Where does the band the Flaming Lips
hail from?
a) Oklahoma
b) Florida
c) Texas
d) California

What are the first names of…
1) Crosby
2) Stills
3) Petty
4) Seger

Who sang "Oh, Pretty Woman" (1964)?
a) The Doors
b) The Ramones
c) Roy Orbison
d) Roy Acuff

Who sang "What's Goin' On" (1971)?
a) Marvin Gaye
b) Michael Bolton
c) Mahalia Jackson
d) Michael Jackson

Who sang "Go Your Own Way" (1976)?

Who sang "When Doves Cry" (1984)?

FUN FACT

The first 12-inch vinyl record
was released in 1931. It was Beethoven's
Fifth Symphony, performed by the
Philadelphia Symphony Orchestra.

Match the member of Kiss to his facial makeup.

1) Gene Simmons   a) Cat face
2) Paul Stanley   b) Stars around both eyes
3) Ace Frehley   c) Star around one eye
4) Peter Cris   d) Wing-ish shapes
                                   around both eyes

Who sang "Born to Run" (1975)?

Who sang "Waterfalls" (1995)?

The president of Czechoslovakia named
what American singer a special ambassador
to the West?
a) Alice Cooper
b) Marilyn Manson
c) Bobby Vinton
d) Frank Zappa

Who sang "Iris" (1998)?

Who sang "Jump" (1984)?

Who sang "Bye Bye Bye" (2000)?

Who sang "Our Lips are Sealed" (1981)?

Who sang "Just the Way You Are" (1977)?

Who sang "Papa Don't Preach" (1986)?

Who sang "Losing My Religion" (1991)?

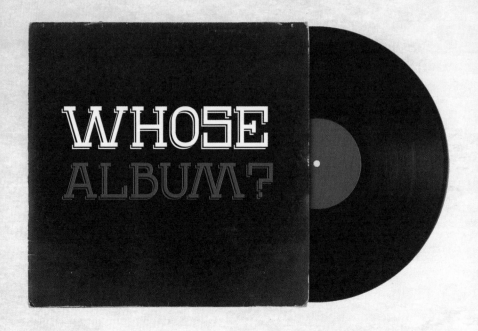

WHOSE ALBUM?

The Monkees or the Beach Boys: Pet Sounds?

Miles Davis or Elvis Presley: Kind of Blue?

**Jimi Hendrix or Janis Joplin:
Are You Experienced?**

Nirvana or Coldplay: Nevermind?

Mac Davis or Fleetwood Mac: Rumors?

B.B. King or Carole King: Tapestry?

Jeff Buckley or Little Richard: Grace?

**Simon and Garfunkel or Stevie Wonder:
Songs in the Key of Life?**

Madonna or the Jayhawks: Something to Remember?

Vampire Weekend or Beck: Sea Change?

**The Avett Brothers or OutKast:
I and Love and You?**

Sufjan Stevens or Wilco: Yankee Hotel Foxtrot?

RAP

On what record label did Kanye West originally produce music for Jay-Z and Alicia Keys?
a) Roc-A-Billy Records
b) Roc-A-Fella Records
c) Roc-Da-House Records
d) Roc-N-Out Records

What record label, run by Kanye West, also recorded John Legend?
a) GREAT Music
b) GOOD Music
c) OKAY Music
d) COOL Music

In what year did Puff Daddy decide to be renamed P. Diddy?
a) 1995
b) 2001
c) 2003
d) 2005

Who did Jay-Z face off with in a 2001 notorious rapping battle?
a) Nas
b) Nose
c) Nus
d) Nise

What numeral is featured twice in the title of an MC Hammer hit?

★ ★

FUN FACT

Dr. Dre was punched in the face
as he was about to receive a
Vibe Lifetime Achievement Award.

★ ★

What group was Lisa "Left-Eye" Lopes
a part of?
a) TLC
b) Run-DMC
c) KRS-One
d) G-Unit

When did Tupac Shakur die?
a) 1990
b) 1996
c) 1998
d) 2000

Who is NOT featured on Drake's
song "Forever"?
a) Kanye West
b) Lil Wayne
c) Eminem
d) Snoop Dogg

Who did Busta Rhymes team up with
on "I Know What You Want"?

HOLIDAY MUSIC

In "The Chipmunk Song," what present does
Alvin really, really want?

What two women are instructed to "bring a torch"
in the title of a Christmas carol?

What are you supposed to go tell
on the mountain?

What does "Gloria in Excelsis Deo"
mean in English?

How many times is Santa checking his list in
the song "Santa Claus Is Comin' to Town"?

What number reindeer is Rudolph?

What is the proper title of the song that begins,
"Chestnuts roasting on an open fire"?

"Away in a Manger" was first published
in 1885 in...
a) Philadelphia
b) London
c) Paris
d) Rome

The lyrics to "Joy to the World"
are taken from...
a) Psalm 92
b) Psalm 98
c) Psalm 114
d) Psalm 122

The lyrics to "O Little Town of Bethlehem"
were written by a...
a) Catholic priest
b) Episcopal priest
c) Baptist minister
d) Lutheran minister

What Christmas song is the best-selling single
(Christmas or otherwise) in history?
a) "All I Want for Christmas Is You"
b) "Do They Know It's Christmas?"
c) "Do You Hear What I Hear?"
d) "White Christmas"

What singer wrote "The Christmas Song" (1943)?
a) Tony Bennett
b) Nat King Cole
c) Dean Martin
d) Mel Tormé

What Broadway composer, best known for
The Music Man, wrote "It's Beginning to Look
a Lot Like Christmas" (1951)?
a) Alan Jay Lerner
b) Richard Rodgers
c) Stephen Sondheim
d) Meredith Willson

What Broadway composer wrote
"White Christmas" (1942)?
a) Harold Arlen
b) Irving Berlin
c) Jerry Herman
d) Richard Rodgers

What movie star narrated the 1970 animated
holiday special *Santa Claus Is Comin' to Town*?
a) Gene Kelly
b) Donald O'Connor
c) Fred Astaire
d) Ginger Rogers

Who played Kris Kringle in the animated
Santa Claus Is Comin' to Town?
a) Mickey Mantle
b) Mickey Rooney
c) Michael Murphy
d) Mitch Miller

In the song "We Wish You a Merry Christmas,"
what treat do the singers demand?
a) Candy canes
b) Cookies
c) Figgy pudding
d) Wassail

★ ★

FUN FACT

A misheard "Rudolph the Red-nosed Reindeer"
lyric led to a best-selling children's book called
"Olive, the Other Reindeer" by Vivian Walsh.

★ ★

MUSIC LIGHTNING ROUND

True or false: "God Bless America" was originally written to be part of a musical comedy revue.

True or false: Francis Scott Key was a prisoner of war when he wrote "The Star Spangled Banner."

True or false: "This Land Is Your Land" was originally called "God Blessed America for Me."

True or false: Bruce Springsteen recorded a version of "This Land Is Your Land."

True or false: The lyrics for "The Star Spangled Banner" come from a poem called "Defense of Fort McHenry."

True or false: "My Country, 'Tis of Thee" has the same melody as the British national anthem "God Save the Queen."

True or false: As a lawyer, Francis Scott Key successfully prosecuted Richard Lawrence, the first man to ever try to assassinate a U.S. president.

True or false: Francis Scott Key is not in the Songwriters Hall of Fame.

True or false: Francis Scott Key and author F. Scott Fitzgerald were distant cousins.

True or false: **There is only one verse to "The Star Spangled Banner."**

True or false: **"God Bless America" originally included the lyric "…to the right with a light from above."**

True or false: **The same person who wrote "You're a Grand Old Flag" wrote "Yankee Doodle Dandy."**

True or false: **"You're a Grand Old Flag" was originally called "You're a Grand Old Rag."**

True or false: **"You're a Grand Old Flag" has the first reference ever to Uncle Sam.**

True or false: **The lyrics to "America the Beautiful" were originally written as a poem called "Pikes Peak."**

True or false: Paul Jabara recorded a disco version of "Yankee Doodle Dandy."

True or false: "The First Noel" was written by Irving Berlin.

True or false: The man credited with naming rock 'n' roll was a deejay in Chicago named Harvey Freed.

True or false: The first album released on CD was by Beethoven.

True or false: Bessie Smith was called "Empress of the Blues."

True or false: The number one pop hit of 1967 was Aretha Franklin's "Respect."

ALABAMA

What are the five states that border the Gulf of Mexico?

In what battle did Admiral David Farragut command, "Damn the torpedoes, full speed ahead"?

The town of Enterprise houses a monument to what destructive insect?

What is the state capital?

What is the state motto?

What is the state tree?

What is the state flower?

What is the state bird?

FUN FACT

Alabama was the first state to declare Christmas a legal holiday.

ALASKA

What is the official state sport?

What is the largest national forest in the United States?

What is Alaska's most valuable natural resource?

What is the state capital?

What is the state motto?

What is the state tree?

What is the state flower?

What is the state bird?

FUN FACT
Alaska is approximately 55 miles from Russia.

ARIZONA

What is Arizona's most abundant mineral?

What river formed the Grand Canyon?

What is the official state neckwear?

What is the state capital?

What is the state motto?

What is the state tree?

What is the state flower?

What is the state bird?

FUN FACT

In Arizona, it's illegal to refuse a person a glass of water.

ARKANSAS

Walmart was founded in 1962 in Rogers, Arkansas, by what man?

What mountainous town is called "The Little Switzerland of the Ozarks"?

What did Bill Clinton and Hillary Rodham teach at the University of Arkansas?

What is the state capital?

What is the state motto?

What is the state tree?

What is the state flower?

What is the state bird?

FUN FACT

Arkansas is the nation's leading producer of both chicken and rice.

CALIFORNIA

Pacific Grove has an unusual law. In this town, it is illegal to molest what annual visitor?

What is the Artichoke Capital of the World?

What high-end chocolatier is headquartered on San Francisco Bay?

What is the state capital?

What is the state motto?

What is the state tree?

What is the state flower?

What is the state bird?

FUN FACT

Mount Shasta is a dormant volcano.

COLORADO

What is Colorado's state nickname?

What's the name of a site of a four-story city carved into cliffs thousands of years ago?

There's only one place in the United States where the corners of four states meet. One of the states is Colorado. What are the other three?

What is the state capital?

What is the state motto?

What is the state tree?

What is the state flower?

What is the state bird?

FUN FACT

Colorado has the highest mean elevation of any state.

CONNECTICUT

Connecticut was the birthplace of what common American food?

The official submarine museum of the United States Navy is in what Connecticut town?

The oldest U.S. newspaper still being published is based in Connecticut. What is it called?

What is the state capital?

What is the state motto?

What is the state tree?

What is the state flower?

What is the state bird?

FUN FACT:

Don't cross the street on your hands in Hartford. It's illegal.

DELAWARE

Delaware has a shared border with another state that goes back to the original land grants from King Charles II and the Duke of York. Which state?

Methodists who purchased land for a summer camp built what is now Delaware's largest beach resort town; what is it?

Delaware has the world's largest population of what aquatic "living fossils"?

What is the state capital?

What is the state motto?

What is the state tree?

What is the state flower?

What is the state bird?

FUN FACT

Delaware was the first state to ratify the U.S. Constitution.

FLORIDA

What Florida city is the nation's oldest permanently occupied European settlement?

What is the largest subtropical wilderness in the United States?

What city is known as the "Venice of America"?

What is the state capital?

What is the state motto?

What is the state tree?

What is the state flower?

What is the state bird?

FUN FACT

Gatorade was named after the University of Florida Gators football team.

GEORGIA

Georgia is the country's top producer of three things that start with the letter P. What are they?

What was invented by Dr. John S. Pemberton in Atlanta, Georgia?

Who wrote *Gone with the Wind*?

What is the state capital?

What is the state motto?

What is the state tree?

What is the state flower?

What is the state bird?

FUN FACT

In Gainesville, Georgia, the Chicken Capital of the World, it is illegal to eat chicken with a fork.

HAWAII

What U.S. Navy deepwater naval base is near Honolulu?

What type of coffee is grown on the leeward side of the Big Island on volcanic slopes?

In Kauai, no building is allowed to be built taller than a _____.

What is the state capital?

What is the state motto?

What is the state tree?

What is the state flower?

What is the state bird?

FUN FACT

Hawaiians eat the most Spam per person in the United States.

IDAHO

Idaho grows one-fourth of what U.S. crop?

What heats the statehouse in Boise?

What is the deepest river gorge in North America, deeper than even the Grand Canyon?

What is the state capital?

What is the state motto?

What is the state tree?

What is the state flower?

What is the state bird?

FUN FACT

While in Idaho, don't fish while sitting on a camel or giraffe. You'd be breaking the law.

ILLINOIS

Where is the world's largest cookie and cracker factory?

What worldwide phenomenon began in Des Plaines, Illinois?

Illinois was the first state to ratify the amendment to abolish _____.

What is the state capital?

What is the state motto?

What is the state tree?

What is the state flower?

What is the state bird?

FUN FACT

Metropolis isn't Superman's hometown; it's a small city in Massac County, Illinois.

INDIANA

What Indiana town gets half a million "Dear Santa" letters a year?

A produce market near Bruceville, Indiana gets attention with a 20-foot-tall _____ next to a replica of the Washington Monument.

The first professional baseball game happened in what Indiana city?

What is the state capital?

What is the state motto?

What is the state tree?

What is the state flower?

What is the state bird?

FUN FACT

The Christmas Story—a holiday tale of BB guns and leg lamps—is based in Indiana.

IOWA

Iowa's eastern and western borders are outlined by what rivers?

What West Branch, Iowa native was the only U.S. President to be born in Iowa?

What is the stage name of Iowa-born film star Marion Morrison?

What is the state capital?

What is the state motto?

What is the state tree?

What is the state flower?

What is the state bird?

FUN FACT

Iowa is the largest producer of corn in the United States.

KANSAS

What worldwide restaurant chain started in Wichita, Kansas?

The first woman to fly solo across the Atlantic Ocean was from Atchison, Kansas. What was her name?

The Reverend Sylvester Graham believed in the health benefits of eating whole-wheat flour. What was named after him?

What is the state capital?

What is the state motto?

What is the state tree?

What is the state flower?

What is the state bird?

FUN FACT

Schlitterbahn Waterpark in Kansas city, Kansas, boasts the tallest waterslide in the world—taller than Niagara Falls.

KENTUCKY

What is the nation's oldest continuously held horse race?

The world's most popular song was written in 1893 by two sisters who taught young children in Louisville. What's the song?

The largest gold reserve in the world is found at what Kentucky institution?

What is the state capital?

What is the state motto?

What is the state tree?

What is the state flower?

What is the state bird?

FUN FACT

The founder of Brown's Chicken was once the governor of Kentucky.

LOUISIANA

Instead of counties, Louisiana's political divisions are called _____.

Louisiana native Rebecca Wells brings the Bayou to life in the novel *Divine Secrets of the* _____ *Sisterhood*.

In 2005, the majority of New Orleans flooded after Hurricane _____.

What is the state capital?

What is the state motto?

What is the state tree?

What is the state flower?

What is the state bird?

FUN FACT

Louisiana state law still refers to the Napoleonic Code.

MAINE

What Maine city is the farthest east in the United States?

What American poet was born in Portland, Maine and was known for the poems "The Courtship of Miles Standish," "Evangeline," and "Hiawatha"?

What Maine seaport became the nation's first incorporated city in 1642?

What is the state capital?

What is the state motto?

What is the state tree?

What is the state flower?

What is the state bird?

FUN FACT

Nine out of ten of the nation's toothpicks are produced in Maine.

MARYLAND

Maryland was the first state to declare an official state sport. What is it?

What unusual beach creatures draw visitors to Assateague Island?

What Maryland city is known as the sailing capital of the world?

What is the state capital?

What is the state motto?

What is the state tree?

What is the state flower?

What is the state bird?

FUN FACT

Greenbelt, Maryland was the first American community built as a planned city.

MASSACHUSETTS

What early governor of Massachusetts is today better known as a brewer?

What's the official state dessert of Massachusetts?

What sport first created in Holyoke, Massachusetts was originally called "Mintonette"?

What is the state capital?

What is the state motto?

What is the state tree?

What is the state flower?

What is the state bird?

FUN FACT

The Fig Newton was named after Newton, Massachusetts.

MICHIGAN

What Michigan city is known as the "Car Capital of the World"?

What's the name of the bridge that connects the upper and lower peninsulas of Michigan, spanning 5 miles?

What U.S. president was a football star at the University of Michigan?

What is the state capital?

What is the state motto?

What is the state tree?

What is the state flower?

What is the state bird?

FUN FACT

Stagecoach Stop No. VI became the city of Novi.

MINNESOTA

What American author lived on Plum Creek
near Walnut Grove?

Minnesotans play what winter sport on ice skates but with
a ball?

What is the only facility in the country to host a World Series,
a Super Bowl, and an NCAA Final Four Basketball
Championship?

What is the state capital?

What is the state motto?

What is the state tree?

What is the state flower?

What is the state bird?

FUN FACT

The Mall of America in Bloomington, Minnesota
is as large as 78 football fields.

MISSISSIPPI

What beverage was invented in Biloxi, Mississippi by Edward Adolf Barq, Sr.?

What toy got its name when Theodore Roosevelt refused to shoot a captured bear on a hunting trip in Mississippi?

What's the name of the 1988 film about civil rights workers going missing in a small Mississippi town?

What is the state capital?

What is the state motto?

What is the state tree?

What is the state flower?

What is the state bird?

FUN FACT

Shoes were first sold as pre-boxed pairs in Vicksburg, Mississippi in 1884.

MISSOURI

Which of the following was **NOT** introduced to the American public at the 1904 St. Louis World's Fair?

A. Waffle cone **B.** Iced tea **C.** Corn dogs **D.** Cotton candy

St. Louis boasts the world's tallest _____.

What is the state capital?

What is the state motto?

What is the state tree?

What is the state flower?

What is the state bird?

FUN FACT

Thousands of couples have tied the knot underground at Bridal Cave in Camdenton, Missouri.

MONTANA

What are Combination, Comet, Black Pine, Pony, and Keystone?

What epic film set in Montana is based on the novella of the same name by Jim Harrison?

What is the state capital?

What is the state motto?

What is the state tree?

What is the state flower?

What is the state bird?

FUN FACT

There are fewer humans in Montana than there are elk, deer, or antelope.

NEBRASKA

Nebraskans enjoy eating a sandwich of sorts, a chewy bread pocket stuffed with beef, onion, and cabbage. What is this called?

Nebraska native Edwin Perkins figured out how to remove liquid from flavor syrup, creating what American drink mix?

What is the state capital?

What is the state motto?

What is the state tree?

What is the state flower?

What is the state bird?

FUN FACT

Whale hunting is prohibited in the landlocked state of Nebraska.

NEVADA

The ichthyosaur is Nevada's official state _____.

From space, what appears to be the brightest neighborhood on earth?

What U.S. silver deposit was discovered in 1859, making Nevada famous?

What is the state capital?

What is the state motto?

What is the state tree?

What is the state flower?

What is the state bird?

FUN FACT

In Las Vegas, it's illegal to pawn your dentures.

Answers: fossil, The Las Vegas Strip, Comstock Lode, Carson City, "All For Our Country," bristlecone pine, sagebrush, mountain bluebird.

NEW HAMPSHIRE

What New Hampshire native founded Christian Science?

What man from East Derry, New Hampshire
was the first American to travel in space?

What is the state capital?

What is the state motto?

What is the state tree?

What is the state flower?

What is the state bird?

FUN FACT

The 1995 Robin Williams blockbuster *Jumanji*
was filmed in Keene, New Hampshire.

NEW  JERSEY

The property names for Monopoly come from what New Jersey location?

What meat is part of a "Jersey breakfast"?

What is the state capital?

What is the state motto?

What is the state tree?

What is the state flower?

What is the state bird?

FUN FACT

New Jersey has more diners per person than any other state. Many are open around the clock.

NEW MEXICO

Every October, Albuquerque hosts the world's largest festival of _____.

When Lew Wallace served as territorial governor in the late 1800s, he wrote a historical novel that was much later made into a movie starring Charleton Heston. What's the novel?

What is the state capital?

What is the state motto?

What is the state tree?

What is the state flower?

What is the state bird?

FUN FACT

Taos Pueblo, a community of multi-story, apartment-like adobe homes has been inhabited for at least 1,000 years—long before Europeans "discovered" America. More than 4,000 people still live there.

NEW YORK

Which president of the United States took the oath of office in New York City?

What is the only American city to host the Winter Olympics twice?

What is the state capital?

What is the state motto?

What is the state tree?

What is the state flower?

What is the state bird?

FUN FACT

Approximately 1 in every 38 people in the United States lives in New York City.

NORTH CAROLINA

Where was the first—although ill-fated—
English colony in America?

What is the oldest state university in the United States?

What sweet restaurant chain was founded
in Winston-Salem?

What is the state capital?

What is the state motto?

What is the state tree?

What is the state flower?

What is the state bird?

FUN FACT

Pepsi was invented in New Bern, North Carolina in 1898

NORTH DAKOTA

The world's largest hamburger was created and consumed in Rutland, North Dakota. Approximately 8,000 people were invited to share the burger. How much did it weigh?

It is illegal do what in North Dakota with shoes on?

What is the state capital?

What is the state motto?

What is the state tree?

What is the state flower?

What is the state bird?

FUN FACT

North Dakota is the least visited state in the United States.

OHIO

What is the official state rock song of Ohio?

In what Ohio city is the Pro Football Hall of Fame located?

What is the state capital?

What is the state motto?

What is the state tree?

What is the state flower?

What is the state bird?

FUN FACT

It is illegal for women to wear patent leather shoes in Ohio. Why? So men can't see the reflection of a woman's underwear in her shoes.

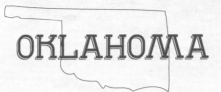

OKLAHOMA

In what decade was John Steinbeck's
The Grapes of Wrath set?

Which Spanish conquistador traveled through the Oklahoma
panhandle looking for the mythical "Seven Cities of Gold?"

What Oklahoma town is named after a number?

What is the state capital?

What is the state motto?

What is the state tree?

What is the state flower?

What is the state bird?

FUN FACT

The movie *Twister* was set in Oklahoma.

OREGON

The deepest lake in the United States was formed by what remains of an ancient volcano. What is the lake called?

What was the longest of the overland routes used in the westward expansion of the United States?

What is the tallest peak in Oregon?

What is the state capital?

What is the state motto?

What is the state tree?

What is the state flower?

What is the state bird?

FUN FACT

The 1985 movie *The Goonies* was filmed mostly in Astoria, Oregon.

PENNSYLVANIA

What famously named animal makes the national news each year as an amateur weather forecaster?

What is the Chocolate Capital of the United States?

Where was the Declaration of Independence signed in 1776?

What is the state capital?

What is the state motto?

What is the state tree?

What is the state flower?

What is the state bird?

FUN FACT

The first U.S. department store, Wanamaker's, was in Philadelphia.

RHODE ISLAND

What man was banished from Plymouth, Massachusetts for "extreme views" regarding freedom of speech and religion and founded Rhode Island?

What era began in Rhode Island in 1790?

What is located 13 miles off the coast of mainland Rhode Island?

What is the state capital?

What is the state motto?

What is the state tree?

What is the state flower?

What is the state bird?

FUN FACT

The first circus in the United States was held in Newport in 1774.

SOUTH CAROLINA

The only major league baseball player to wear the name of his hometown on his uniform was pitcher Bill Voiselle. What was his number?

Where was the first battle of the Civil War?

What stretches 60 miles from Little River, South Carolina, to Georgetown, South Carolina?

What is the state capital?

What is the state motto?

What is the state tree?

What is the state flower?

What is the state bird?

FUN FACT

In 1969, the Cremora factory in Chester, South Carolina, developed exhaust vent issues and rained powdered, non-dairy creamer onto the town.

SOUTH DAKOTA

What world-famous mountain carving is in South Dakota?

What national park contains the world's richest Oligocene epoch fossil beds, dating 23 to 35 million years old?

The United States acquired the region known as South Dakota as part of the _____ in 1803?

What is the state capital?

What is the state motto?

What is the state tree?

What is the state flower?

What is the state bird?

FUN FACT

Mitchell, South Dakota has a Corn Palace built with thousands of bushels of ear corn.

TENNESSEE

What is the world's longest continuously running live radio program, broadcast every Friday and Saturday night since 1925?

What is the Elvis Presley estate in Memphis called?

What Tennessee native became President of the United States when Abraham Lincoln was assassinated?

What is the state capital?

What is the state motto?

What is the state tree?

What is the state flower?

What is the state bird?

FUN FACT

The Dolly Parton Parkway takes visitors to Great Smoky Mountains National Park.

TEXAS

Texas Governor James Hogg requested that a certain tree be planted by his grave instead of a headstone. It became his state tree 13 years later. What is this "nutty" tree?

The bowie knife is named after Jim Bowie, who was a hero in what battle?

What is the official state sport of Texas?

What is the state capital?

What is the state motto?

What is the state flower?

What is the state bird?

FUN FACT

Sweetwater, Texas hosts the world's largest rattlesnake roundup every spring.

UTAH

What is the largest natural lake west of the Mississippi River?

Utah is the most homogeneous state in terms of religion. About 62 percent the people of Utah are what faith?

What is the state capital?

What is the state motto?

What is the state tree?

What is the state flower?

What is the state bird?

FUN FACT

The nation's leading manufacturer of rubber chickens is in Salt Lake City, Utah.

VERMONT

What Vermont-based ice cream company gives their waste to local hog farmers?

What U.S. President was born on the Fourth of July in Plymouth, Vermont?

With more than 500,000 gallons a year, Vermont is the nation's largest producer of _____.

What is the state capital?

What is the state motto?

What is the state tree?

What is the state flower?

What is the state bird?

FUN FACT

The Von Trapp family that escaped Austria, as depicted in the film *The Sound of Music*, moved to Stowe, Vermont, which reminded them of the Alps.

VIRGINIA

Monticello was the home of which U.S. President?

What is the largest office building in the world?

What is the state capital?

What is the state motto?

What is the state tree?

What is the state flower?

What is the state bird?

FUN FACT

A Virginia Chinese restaurant installed a bulletproof window because it was a favorite place for George W. Bush to eat.

Answers: Thomas Jefferson, the Pentagon, Richmond, "Sic semper tyrannis" (in Latin: "Thus always to tyrants"), flowering dogwood, dogwood, cardinal.

WASHINGTON

What was the deadliest volcanic event in the history of the United States?

Washington State is home to the world's largest aircraft maker, which is _____.

What is the state capital?

What is the state motto?

What is the state tree?

What is the state flower?

What is the state bird?

FUN FACT

The widely known and loved (or hated) company Starbucks was founded in Seattle.

WEST VIRGINIA

Three-quarters of the nation's supply of _____ comes from West Virginia.

What percentage of West Virginia is covered by forests?

What legendary part-human/part-insect beast is the subject of a spooky 12-foot steel statue in Point Pleasant, West Virginia?

What is the state capital?

What is the state motto?

What is the state tree?

What is the state flower?

What is the state bird?

FUN FACT

Weirton, West Virginia is the only city in the U. S. that extends from one state border to another.

WISCONSIN

What iconic doll lives in a fictional Wisconsin town?

What is known as the "the world's stinkiest cheese" and, within the United States, is only produced in Monroe County, Wisconsin?

What is the state capital?

What is the state motto?

What is the state tree?

What is the state flower?

What is the state bird?

FUN FACT

Wisconsin has 16,692 lakes.

WYOMING

What is depicted on the Wyoming license plate?

Cody, Wyoming is named after what outlaw?

What was the first official national park?

What is the state capital?

What is the state motto?

What is the state tree?

What is the state flower?

What is the state bird?

FUN FACT

James Cash Penney opened the first J.C. Penney store in Kemmerer, Wyoming in 1902.

Answers: a man on a bucking bronco, William "Buffalo Bill" Cody, Yellowstone, Cheyenne, "Equal Rights," cottonwood, Indian paint brush, Wisconsin meadowlark.

If you have enjoyed this book
or it has touched your life in some way,
we would love to hear from you.

Please send your comments to:
Hallmark Book Feedback
P.O. Box 419034
Mail Drop 100
Kansas City, MO 64141

Or e-mail us at:
booknotes@hallmark.com